EXTREME ANIMALS

BRILLIANT BIRDS

Isabel Thomas

Raintree

www.raintreepublishers.co.uk
Visit our website to find out
more information about
Raintree books.

To order:
☎ Phone 0845 6044371
🖹 Fax +44 (0) 1865 312263
🖳 Email myorders@raintreepublishers.co.uk

Customers from outside the UK please telephone +44 1865 312262

Raintree is an imprint of Capstone Global Library
Limited, a company incorporated in England and Wales
having its registered office at 7 Pilgrim Street, London,
EC4V 6LB – Registered company number: 6695582

Edited by Daniel Nunn, John-Paul Wilkins,
  and Rebecca Rissman
Designed by Philippa Jenkins
Picture research by Elizabeth Alexander
Production by Victoria Fitzgerald
Originated by Capstone Global Library
Printed and bound in China by CTPS

ISBN 978 1 406 23776 4
16 15 14 13
10 9 8 7 6 5 4 3 2

British Library Cataloguing in Publication Data
Thomas, Isabel
Brilliant birds. -- (Extreme animals)
598-dc22
A full catalogue record for this book is available from
the British Library.

Acknowledgements
We would like to thank the following for permission
to reproduce photographs: © Jolyon Troscianko p. 22;
Alamy p. 27 (© Frans Lanting Studio); iStockphoto
pp. 9 (© Bob Balestri), 15 (© Tobias Müller), 20 (©
ChristianWilkinson), 25 (© Patrycja Zboch); Nature
Picture Library pp. 8 (© Rolf Nussbaumer), 23 (© Miles
Barton); Photolibrary pp. 12 (Antoine Dervaux/Bios),
14 (Michel & Christine Denis-Huot/Bios), 17 (Konrad
Wothe/OSF), 21 (Mark Jones/Age footstock), 26 (Mark
Carwardine/Peter Arnold Images); Photoshot p. 18
(imagebroker/Ulrich Doering); Shutterstock pp. 4 (©
Tom Davison), 5 (© Borislav Borisov), 6 (© Luiz Claudio
Ribeiro), 7 (© Graeme Shannon), 10 (© John
Carnemolla), 11 (© Roadworks), 13 (© Christian Musat),
16 (© EcoPrint), 19 (© Dmitry_Tsvetkov), 24 (©
Vishnevskiy Vasily).

Main cover photograph of pink flamingo reproduced
with permission of Shutterstock (© FER737NG).
Background cover photograph of feathers reproduced
with permission of Shutterstock (© Naomi Hasegawa).

Every effort has been made to contact copyright
holders of material reproduced in this book. Any
omissions will be rectified in subsequent printings if
notice is given to the publisher.

Disclaimer
All the Internet addresses (URLs) given in this book were
valid at the time of going to press. However, due to the
dynamic nature of the Internet, some addresses may
have changed, or sites may have changed or ceased to
exist since publication. While the author and publisher
regret any inconvenience this may cause readers, no
responsibility for any such changes can be accepted by
either the author or the publisher.

Some words are shown in bold, **like this**. You can find
out what they mean by looking in the glossary.

Contents

Extreme birds 4

Regal eagles 6

Helicopter hummingbirds 8

Outsized ostriches 10

Tough penguins. 12

Revolting vultures 14

Bird builders and artists. 16

Fearless flamingos 18

Soaring albatrosses. 20

Cunning crows 22

Tongue-twisting woodpeckers 24

Noisy kakapos 26

Record-breakers 28

Glossary. .30

Find out more 31

Index 32

Extreme birds

Think you know everything about birds? Think again! All birds have wings and feathers. But the differences between birds are what make them **extreme**.

Some birds have bizarre bodies. Some behave in weird ways. These features help them to find **mates** or food – or avoid getting eaten themselves!

Extreme colours help some male birds to attract female birds.

DID YOU KNOW?
Bee-eaters can remove a bee's sting before eating it!

Regal eagles

Champion human weightlifters can lift one-and-a-half times their body weight. This is nothing compared to eagle power. Some eagles can carry monkeys or deer four times their weight!

DID YOU KNOW?

Eagles attack and eat anything they can carry, including snakes!

huge eyes to spot **prey**

sharp **talons**

7

Helicopter hummingbirds

How long would it take you to flap your arms 90 times? Some hummingbirds can flap their wings 90 times in 1 second! This helps them to **hover** in front of flowers.

DID YOU KNOW?

Hummingbirds need lots of energy. They eat every 10 minutes, and visit up to 1,500 flowers every day.

long beak for reaching **nectar** inside flowers

Bee hummingbirds are just 57 millimetres long. That is smaller than many rainforest butterflies!
actual size

Outsized ostriches

Ostriches are the world's biggest birds. They are too heavy to fly, but they don't need to. They can run at more than 70 kilometres an hour – fast enough to escape most **predators**. Each stride can be as long as two cars!

big muscles for running

world's largest
eggs

11

Tough penguins

Emperor penguins survive the world's worst weather in the **Antarctic**. Icy **blizzards** make it feel three times colder than a freezer! Each male spends the winter looking after an egg. If a penguin drops its egg, the chick inside will freeze to death in two minutes.

Male Emperor penguins huddle together to keep warm in the freezing cold.

DID YOU KNOW?
Penguins have spiky tongues. This helps the birds to grip slippery fish.

Revolting vultures

When **predators** like lions kill an animal, they leave the most disgusting bits behind. Vultures find this rotting meat and gobble it up! They eat so much that it becomes difficult for them to fly.

DID YOU KNOW?

Egyptian vultures use rocks to break open ostrich eggs.

Vultures stick their heads deep inside dead animals. Being bald means they get less blood and gore stuck to their heads!

Bird builders and artists

Weaver birds build the world's largest nests. The nests are like blocks of flats, with room for hundreds of birds. Living together protects the birds from **predators**.

nest

Male bowerbirds are artists. They make beautiful displays with flowers, leaves, and other pretty things. They want to impress female bowerbirds.

plastic spoon

feathers

bottle top

Fearless flamingos

This lake is hot, stinky, and poisonous. The water would kill most animals. But flamingos can feed safely here. They have special **bills** that **filter** food from the water.

A flock of flamingos can contain up to one million birds.

ankle

19

Soaring albatrosses

Albatrosses hunt, eat, and sleep at sea. Some don't set foot on land for 10 years at a time.

An albatross can fly for days without flapping its huge wings. It uses energy from wind to stay in the air.

DID YOU KNOW?
Scientists have **tagged** albatrosses to find out how far they fly. One albatross flew around the world in 46 days.

21

Cunning crows

Crows are very clever. They think like humans! They are the only birds that can invent new tools. They make hooks from sticks and leaves. They use their tools to scoop insects from small holes.

23

Tongue - twisting woodpeckers

Imagine that your tongue reached your knees! A woodpecker's tongue is two-thirds the length of its body. It uses its tongue to grab food from holes in trees. The tip of its tongue can sense **vibrations** made by moving insects.

25

Noisy kakapos

Kakapos are the fattest parrots in the world. Males make a booming sound to attract females. The noise can be heard up to 5 kilometres away!

The male kakapo sucks in air until he is as big as a football. Then he releases a deep boom. He does this all night, every night for two or three months!

Record-breakers

Which bird do you think is the most **extreme**? Why? Have a look at some of these record-breaking birds to help you decide.

What? Common swift

Why? Longest flight without stopping

Wow! When swifts leave their nests for the first time, they fly non-stop for two years. They can travel 500,000 kilometres in one go. That's further away than the Moon!

What? Ruppell's vulture

Why? Highest flying bird

Wow! This high flyer has been spotted at a height of 11,278 metres. That's high enough to peer into the windows of a jumbo jet!

What? Albatross

Why? Longest wings

Wow! The wandering albatross has wings that measure more than 3.5 metres from tip to tip. That's like 17 footballs in a row!

What? Peregrine falcon

Why? Fastest flying bird

Wow! When chasing **prey**, Peregrine falcons dive-bomb at speeds of 250 kilometres an hour!

What? Ostrich

Why? Largest bird's egg

Wow! One ostrich egg can weigh as much as 24 chicken eggs!

What? Kakapo

Why? Longest-living bird

Wow! No bird has more birthdays than a kakapo. These parrots can live for more than 100 years!

Antarctic land or seas at or near the South Pole

bill hard mouth part of a bird or other animal

blizzard long, heavy snowstorm

extreme unusual, amazing, or different from normal

filter remove or separate from liquid

hover stay hanging in the air

mates two animals that can have baby animals together

nectar sweet, sugary liquid made by flowers

predator animal that hunts other animals for food

prey animal that is hunted by another animal for food

tagged fitted with a tiny radio that tells scientists where the animal is

talon claw of an eagle or other bird of prey

vibrations small back and forth movements that make a noise

Find out more

Books

Beastly Birds and Bats, Lynne Huggins-Cooper (QEB Publishing, 2008)

Birds of Prey (Wild Predators), Andrew Solway (Raintree, 2005)

RSPB First Book of Birds, Anita Ganeri (A & C Black, 2011)

Websites

Help to protect amazing kakapos:
www.kakaporecovery.org.nz/

Learn more about birds and animals of all kinds:
www.rspb.org.uk/youth/

Become a hummingbird in ZSL London Zoo's online game:
www.zsl.org/kids

albatrosses 20–21, 29

bee hummingbirds 9
bee-eaters 5
bowerbirds 17

crows 22–23

eagles 6–7
eggs 11, 12, 14, 29
Emperor penguins 12

flamingos 18–19
flying 20, 21, 28, 29
food 5, 6, 8, 14, 15,
   18, 22, 23

hummingbirds 8–9

kakapos 26–27, 29

nectar 8
nests 16

ostriches 10–11, 14, 29

parrots 26–27, 29
penguins 12–13
peregrine falcons 29
predators 10, 14, 16
prey 6, 7

Ruppell's vultures 28

swifts 28

talons 7
tongues 13, 24, 25
tools 22

vultures 14–16, 28

weaver birds 16
wings 8, 29
woodpeckers 24–25